THE MIAMI MARLINS

BY
MARK STEWART

NORWOOD HOUSE  PRESS

CHICAGO, ILLINOIS

Norwood House Press
P.O. Box 316598
Chicago, Illinois 60631

For information regarding Norwood House Press, please visit our website at:
www.norwoodhousepress.com or call 866-565-2900.

All photos courtesy of Getty Images except the following:
Tom DiPace (4, 8, 11), Black Book Partners Archives (6, 9, 10, 22, 23, 25, 27, 28, 34 bottom left,
35 top left & right, 36, 37, 38, 43 both, 45), Pinnacle Brands (7), Associated Press (12, 14),
Topps, Inc. (15, 21, 34 bottom right, 35 bottom right, 40, 42 top & bottom left),
Author's Collection (33), Matt Richman (48).
Cover Photo: Associated Press

The memorabilia and artifacts pictured in this book are presented for educational and informational purposes,
and come from the collection of the author.

Editor: Mike Kennedy
Designer: Ron Jaffe
Project Management: Black Book Partners, LLC.
Special thanks to Topps, Inc.

Library of Congress Cataloging-in-Publication Data

Stewart, Mark, 1960-
  The Miami Marlins / by Mark Stewart.
     p. cm. -- (Team spirit)
  Includes bibliographical references and index.
  Summary: "A Team Spirit Baseball edition featuring the Miami Marlins that
chronicles the history and accomplishments of the team. Includes access to
the Team Spirit website, which provides additional information, updates and
photos"--Provided by publisher.
  ISBN 978-1-59953-482-4 (library : alk. paper) -- ISBN 978-1-60357-362-7
(ebook) 1. Miami Marlins (Baseball team)--History--Juvenile literature. 2.
Florida Marlins (Baseball team)--History--Juvenile literature. I. Title.
  GV875.M47S74 2012
  796.357'6409759381--dc23

                                              2011048494

Manufactured in the United States of America in North Mankato, Minnesota.
196N—012012

COVER PHOTO: The Miami Marlins show off their new uniforms prior to the 2012 season.

TABLE OF CONTENTS

CHAPTER	PAGE
MEET THE MARLINS	4
GLORY DAYS	6
HOME TURF	12
DRESSED FOR SUCCESS	14
WE WON!	16
GO-TO GUYS	20
CALLING THE SHOTS	24
ONE GREAT DAY	26
LEGEND HAS IT	28
IT REALLY HAPPENED	30
TEAM SPIRIT	32
TIMELINE	34
FUN FACTS	36
TALKING BASEBALL	38
GREAT DEBATES	40
FOR THE RECORD	42
PINPOINTS	44
GLOSSARY	46
EXTRA INNINGS	47
INDEX	48

ABOUT OUR GLOSSARY

In this book, there may be several words that you are reading for the first time. Some are sports words, some are new vocabulary words, and some are familiar words that are used in an unusual way. All of these words are defined on page 46. Throughout the book, sports words appear in **bold type**. Regular vocabulary words appear in *bold italic type*.

MEET THE MARLINS

A marlin is a swift, powerful fish that moves through the water with great confidence in search of its next meal. That is also a good way to describe the Miami Marlins. They gobble up opponents with tremendous power and speed. They play every game with maximum effort.

The Marlins do their hunting on the baseball diamond, of course. They are always on the lookout for young talent to blend with experienced stars. In their most successful seasons, this has been the winning recipe.

This book tells the story of the Marlins. While most teams depend on a small group of stars, Miami is at its best when everyone on the team has a chance to play. That is why, even when the odds are against them, the Marlins are never really out of a game. On any given day, any player can win a game and be a hero.

Gaby Sanchez gets a high-five from Hanley Ramirez. The Marlins have been most successful when building around young stars like these two.

I n 1993, the **National League (NL)** decided it was time to add two new teams. One of them would be in Florida. Groups from different cities around the state made their "pitch" to get that team. The winner was Miami. However, instead of using the city's name, the team's new ownership chose to call the club the Florida Marlins. This way, everyone in the state would think of the Marlins as their team.

Over the next 19 seasons, the Marlins gave their fans plenty to get excited about. The team assembled a talented roster in its early years, including **All-Stars** Jeff Conine, Gary Sheffield, Charles Johnson, and Robb Nen. Unfortunately, the Marlins often struggled. That began to change in 1996 when Kevin Brown, Al Leiter, and Devon White joined the club. A year later, the Marlins added Moises Alou, Alex Fernandez, and Bobby Bonilla.

LEFT: Gary Sheffield set a team record with 42 homers in 1996.
RIGHT: Edgar Renteria was a young leader on the 1997 Marlins.

At the same time, young players such as Edgar Renteria, Luis Castillo, Craig Counsell, and Livan Hernandez began to *contribute*. The Marlins went from having a losing record in their first four seasons to winning the **World Series** in 1997. They beat the Cleveland Indians in one of the most thrilling finishes ever.

After the World Series, team owner Wayne Huizenga broke up the team by trading away many of his best—and highest-paid—players. Unhappy with Huizenga's moves, many fans stayed away from the ballpark. In 1999, Huizenga decided he would rather be a baseball fan than a team owner and sold the Marlins.

Florida soon dropped in the **standings**. From 1998 to 2002, the team had a losing record every year. However, the Marlins slowly rebuilt their roster with exciting young players. They had a group of hard-throwing pitchers, including Brad Penny, A.J. Burnett,

Carl Pavano, Josh Beckett, and Braden Looper. They also had some very good hitters, including Derrek Lee, Mike Lowell, and Juan Pierre.

In 2003, the team signed All-Star catcher Ivan Rodriguez to handle the young **pitching staff**. The Marlins also called up Miguel Cabrera and Dontrelle Willis from the **minor leagues**. Rodriguez, Cabrera, and Willis gave the team a spark. After starting the year slowly, the Marlins finished strong and made the **playoffs** as the NL **Wild Card**. Against all odds, they won the **pennant** and beat the powerful New York Yankees in the World Series.

Amazing as it may seem, the Marlins had just two winning seasons in their first 11 years. Yet both times they ended up as champions of baseball. The experts learned an important lesson from Florida's formula for success. If you put the right players in the right places at just the right time, great things can happen.

In the years after their 2003 championship, the Marlins found more good young players and also made a lot of smart trades. They sent Beckett to the Boston Red Sox in exchange for Hanley Ramirez and Anibal Sanchez. Ramirez was named **Rookie of the Year** in

LEFT: Hanley Ramirez was the NL batting champion in 2009.
ABOVE: Juan Pierre stole 167 bases in his three seasons with the Marlins.

2006 and won the NL batting championship in 2009. Sanchez threw a **no-hitter** in 2006 and almost threw two more in 2011.

In 2005, the Marlins saw something special in an unwanted infielder named Dan Uggla. They plucked him off the roster of the Arizona Diamondbacks and made him their starting second baseman. Uggla soon became an All-Star. Two years later, the Marlins convinced 17-year-old Mike Stanton to turn down a generous college *scholarship* in order to play for them. By 2012, he was one of the top power hitters in the sport.

ABOVE: The Marlins gave Dan Uggla a chance when no one else would.
RIGHT: Mike Stanton watches a hit go toward the left field fence.

The 2012 season also marked a new era for the team. After nearly two **decades** as the Florida Marlins, the club renamed itself the Miami Marlins. They made a big splash by signing several **free agents**, including All-Stars Jose Reyes, Heath Bell, and Mark Buehrle. This **strategy** had worked well in the past.

The Marlins also moved into a new stadium, built close to downtown Miami. With two World Series championships in their brief history, they have a **reputation** for building exciting teams. It may not be long before the Marlins add more trophies to their case.

HOME TURF

For their first 19 seasons, the Marlins played in a stadium located in Miami Gardens, a town just north of the city of Miami. The stadium was built for the Miami Dolphins football team, but the field was made extra-wide to fit baseball and soccer games as well. The Marlins' stadium had one of the deepest outfields in baseball. It was very hard to hit home runs there, especially to center field.

In 2012, the team moved into a beautiful new ballpark, which was designed specifically for baseball. The stadium's most notable feature is a *retractable* roof. It allows games to be played no matter what the weather is outside. Like the team's old stadium, the new ballpark is a dream for pitchers because it also has a very big outfield.

BY THE NUMBERS

- *The Marlins' stadium has 37,000 seats.*
- *The distance from home plate to the left field foul pole is 340 feet.*
- *The distance from home plate to the center field wall is 416 feet.*
- *The distance from home plate to the right field foul pole is 335 feet.*

Billy the Marlin watches as workers put the finishing touches on the team's new field to get it ready for Opening Day.

DRESSED FOR SUCCESS

In the Marlins' first season, they used a combination of teal and black as their colors. Teal mixes green and blue, which reminded many people of ocean water. Sometimes the Marlins wore a sleeveless jersey, and the t-shirt they slipped on underneath their top was teal. In 1996, the team switched to black as its primary color. The Marlins have also used a *pinstripe* uniform design.

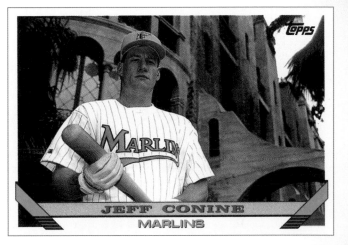

JEFF CONINE
MARLINS

In 2012, the Marlins introduced a new uniform and *logo*. Blue, red-orange, and yellow became their main colors. The team wanted fans to think of the sun setting over the sea when they watched the Marlins play. The team also replaced the *F* on its caps with an *M* for Miami. The lettering was very thick, which worked well with the new logo. Now it shows a marlin swimming above an *M*.

LEFT: Josh Johnson models one of the team's 2012 home uniforms.
ABOVE: Jeff Conine poses for his 1993 trading card in the team's first uniform with pinstripes.

WE WON!

I n baseball, teams that pull together under pressure have the best chance of winning a championship. There is no better example of this than the Marlins. In 1997, and again in 2003, they found the right mix of hitting, pitching, and fielding to rise to the top of baseball. Both years, they were crowned World Series champions. Both years, they entered the playoffs as a Wild Card team—no one really thought they had a chance.

In 1997, the Marlins finished far behind the Atlanta Braves in the **NL East**. But Florida made it to the playoffs thanks to experienced players such as Kevin Brown, Al Leiter, Gary Sheffield, Jeff Conine, Devon White, Bobby Bonilla, Darren Daulton, and Moises Alou. They were joined by young stars Edgar Renteria, Charles Johnson, Robb Nen, Alex Fernandez, and Livan Hernandez.

LEFT: Jim Leyland congratulates Livan Hernandez after a playoff victory.
RIGHT: Charles Johnson and Kevin Brown discuss the next hitter.

Despite the odds against his team, manager Jim Leyland got the Marlins believing they could do anything. In any game, any player felt like he could be a hero. In the first round of the playoffs, Florida swept the San Francisco Giants in three games. Against the Braves in the **National League Championship Series (NLCS)**, Brown and Hernandez won two games each. The Marlins batted just .199 as a team, but they got **clutch** hits when they needed them. Hernandez struck out 15 hitters in Game 5 and was named the **Most Valuable Player (MVP)** of the series.

Florida faced the Cleveland Indians in the 1997 World Series. Both teams hit well, and the series seesawed back and forth. In the exciting Game 7, the Indians led 2–1 in the bottom of the ninth inning. Craig Counsell, who was playing in place of injured Luis Castillo, tied the game. Two innings later, Counsell was standing on third base

with two outs. Renteria, Florida's youngest player, drove him home with a single to center field. The Marlins were champions!

Six years later, the Marlins were up to their old tricks. Once again, the Braves had a big lead in the NL East, and once again the Marlins played just well enough to make the playoffs as the Wild Card. Florida was a very young team. Catcher Ivan Rodriguez was the only everyday player over the age of 30.

As in 1997, the 2003 Marlins had a new hero every day. Derrek Lee, Miguel Cabrera, and Mike Lowell supplied power. Juan Pierre and Castillo gave the team great speed. Josh Beckett, Dontrelle Willis, Brad Penny, and Carl Pavano anchored a good pitching staff. Manager Jack McKeon never seemed to make a wrong decision.

The Marlins beat the Giants and the Chicago Cubs in the playoffs to win the pennant. They were behind in both series, but each time they found a way to win. Against the Cubs in the NLCS, Florida was just six outs away from losing. The Marlins scored eight runs in the eighth inning to win Game 6 and pounded Chicago's pitching in Game 7 for two remarkable victories.

In the World Series, Pierre's speed helped the Marlins beat the New York Yankees in Game 1. After losing the next two games, the Marlins tied the series when shortstop Alex Gonzalez hit a home run in the bottom of the 12th inning of Game 4.

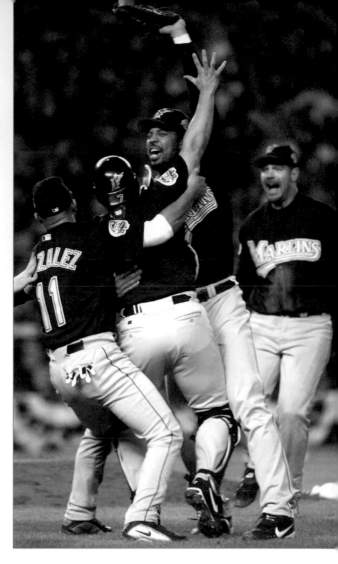

The Marlins won Game 5, and then sent Beckett to the mound for Game 6. Though he had pitched against the Yankees just three days earlier, he was ready to face New York again. In one of the greatest pitching performances ever, Beckett overpowered the Yankees for nine innings and won 2–0. The Marlins were champions again!

LEFT: Brad Penny fires a pitch toward home plate.   **ABOVE**: Derrek Lee raises his arm in triumph after the Marlins beat the New York Yankees.

GO-TO GUYS

To be a true star in baseball, you need more than a quick bat and a strong arm. You have to be a "go-to guy"—someone the manager wants on the pitcher's mound or in the batter's box when it matters most. Fans of the Marlins have had a lot to cheer about over the years, including these great stars …

THE PIONEERS

JEFF CONINE   Outfielder/First Baseman

• BORN: 6/27/1966

• PLAYED FOR TEAM: 1993 TO 1997 & 2003 TO 2005

Jeff Conine was the Marlins' most dependable player in their early years. He was a good hitter and leader who came to the ballpark ready to play every day. Conine was an All-Star twice.

GARY SHEFFIELD   Outfielder

• BORN: 11/18/1968

• PLAYED FOR TEAM: 1993 TO 1998

Gary Sheffield was an infielder before he joined the Marlins. The team needed a slugger in the outfield, so he agreed to move to a new position. In 1996, Sheffield hit 42 home runs and drove in 120 runs.

LUIS CASTILLO

Second Baseman

- BORN: 9/12/1975
- PLAYED FOR TEAM: 1996 TO 2005

Luis Castillo was one of the fastest players in baseball when he played for the Marlins. He led the NL in stolen bases twice. In 2000, Castillo batted .334 and had 62 steals.

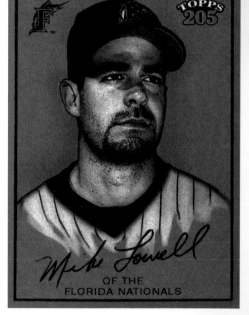

MIKE LOWELL

Third Baseman

- BORN: 2/24/1974
- PLAYED FOR TEAM: 1999 TO 2005

The Marlins got Mike Lowell in a trade with the New York Yankees. In 2003, he led the Marlins with 32 home runs and 105 **runs batted in (RBIs)**. Lowell then helped the team beat New York in the World Series.

JOSH BECKETT

Pitcher

- BORN: 5/15/1980   • PLAYED FOR TEAM: 2001 TO 2005

Josh Beckett grew up in Texas idolizing superstars Nolan Ryan and Roger Clemens, who were also Texans. In 2003, Beckett did something that neither of his idols had done—he pitched a **shutout** to win the World Series.

ABOVE: Mike Lowell

DONTRELLE WILLIS   Pitcher

- BORN: 1/12/1982   • PLAYED FOR TEAM: 2003 TO 2007

When Dontrelle Willis joined the Marlins, fans all over the country fell in love with him and jammed into ballparks whenever he pitched. Willis had an unusual pitching style, a great attitude, and an amazing fastball.

MIGUEL CABRERA   Third Baseman/Outfielder

- BORN: 4/18/1983

- PLAYED FOR TEAM: 2003 TO 2007

Miguel Cabrera had just turned 20 when the Marlins made him an everyday player in 2003. Cabrera gave them a powerful bat in the middle of the batting order. In five seasons with the team, he had more than 500 RBIs.

JOSH JOHNSON   Pitcher

- BORN: 1/31/1984

- FIRST YEAR WITH TEAM: 2005

Marlins fans knew Josh Johnson was something special the moment he joined the club. He threw hard and had tremendous control. In 2010, Johnson led the NL with an **earned run average (ERA)** of 2.30 and struck out 186 batters in 183 innings.

ABOVE: Miguel Cabrera   **RIGHT**: Hanley Ramirez

HANLEY RAMIREZ   Shortstop

- BORN: 12/23/1983
- FIRST YEAR WITH TEAM: 2006

Very few shortstops can "do it all." Hanley Ramirez was one of them. In his first four years with the Marlins, Ramirez won a batting championship, led the league in runs, stole 51 bases (twice!), and hit more than 100 home runs.

DAN UGGLA   Second Baseman

- BORN: 3/11/1980
- PLAYED FOR TEAM: 2006 TO 2010

Second basemen are normally good fielders and fast runners who hit with little power. Dan Uggla gave the Marlins muscle at the position. He hit over 30 home runs four years in a row.

MIKE STANTON   Outfielder

- BORN: 11/8/1989   • FIRST YEAR WITH TEAM: 2010

Mike Stanton joined the Marlins at the age of 20. Soon he was one of the most feared sluggers in baseball. In 2011, Stanton hit a ball into a section of the Marlins' stadium that was closed off to fans—because it was too far away from home plate!

Many baseball fans think of the Marlins as a "new" team. Perhaps that is the reason why they like to hire experienced managers. Their first manager, Rene Lachemann, had been a coach for four pennant winners in the **American League (AL)**. He taught the young Marlins the basics of baseball. John Boles followed Lachemann

and took two turns managing the team. He showed the Marlins the value of hard work in 2006.

The manager who brought Florida its first championship was Jim Leyland. He was very good at mixing the talents of his players. In turn, they respected Leyland and played hard for him. The same was true of Jack McKeon. He managed the team to its 2003 championship. Though McKeon was in his seventies, he did a great job with Florida's young players. Joe Girardi took over for McKeon and was named Manager of the Year.

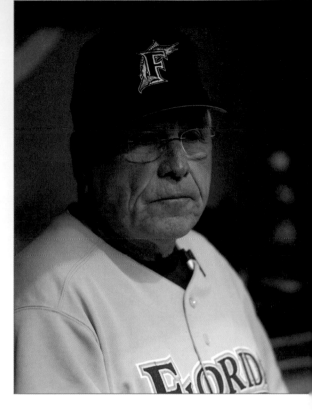

LEFT: Jim Leyland
RIGHT: Jack McKeon

In 2011, Marlins fans were a little surprised—and very happy—to see McKeon return to the dugout. The team had begun the season with a bad losing streak. The Marlins asked McKeon to come back and save the club as he had eight years earlier. Once again, he gave young players lots of responsibility. The team gained confidence and played well the rest of the year. This helped build a foundation for the future.

McKeon was 80 when he returned to the dugout in Miami. Some said he was too old to manage again. But baseball was in his blood. "I don't need this job," McKeon said after he was rehired by the Marlins. "But I love it."

As planned, McKeon stepped down after the 2011 season. Miami hired Ozzie Guillen to take his place. Guillen had been a coach on the Marlins' 2003 World Series team. He left to manage the Chicago White Sox and led that club to a championship in 2005. The Marlins believed Guillen's "homecoming" would help them return to the World Series in the years to come.

ONE GREAT DAY

Unlike other sports, time never "runs out" on a baseball game. Teams play until the final out is made. Marlins fans learned this lesson during the 2003 National League Championship Series. The Marlins and Chicago Cubs met that fall to decide the pennant. Florida trailed after five games. Game 6 was played in Chicago's Wrigley Field. Fans love this ballpark because they can sit very close to the players.

In the eighth inning, the Cubs led 3–0. The celebration was already beginning in Chicago. The Cubs had not been to the World Series since 1945. Back in Florida, many fans turned off their TVs. They could not bear to watch the final outs of the season.

With one out and a runner on first, Luis Castillo lifted a pop-up down the left field line. Moises Alou—a World Series hero for the Marlins in 1997—drifted over to the stands to catch the ball. Several fans stood up and also reached for the ball. One *deflected* it away from Alou.

Luis Castillo's pop-up started a wild chain of events for the Marlins in 2003.

Suddenly the Marlins had new life. Castillo walked, and Ivan Rodriguez followed with a single to make the score 3–1. Miguel Cabrera came to bat and hit a ground ball that was perfect for a double play. But the Cubs made an error, and everyone was safe. Derrek Lee was up next. He smacked a double to tie the game.

The Marlins scored five more runs in the inning. The big blow came off the bat of little-used Mike Mordecai. The 35-year-old part-time player hit a double with the bases loaded. All three runners scored. The Cubs and their fans were in shock. The Marlins won 8–3. They won Game 7, too. And 10 days later, the Marlins defeated the New York Yankees to become World Series champions.

LEGEND HAS IT

WHICH MARLIN HAD THE BEST COLLECTION OF BOBBLEHEAD DOLLS?

LEGEND HAS IT that Miguel Cabrera did. He had old bobbleheads and new ones, and bobbleheads of many of his Florida teammates. His most prized bobbleheads were the 1997 versions of Jeff Conine and Craig Counsell. Cabrera got them as a fan when he went to a Marlins game. The team completed his collection—and made Cabrera's day—when they gave away a Miguel Cabrera bobblehead during a 2005 game.

ABOVE: Miguel Cabrera collected hits and bobbleheads when he played for the Marlins.

HAVE THE MARLINS EVER LOST TO A ROCK BAND?

LEGEND HAS IT that they did. In 2011, a concert by the popular rock band U2 was scheduled in the Marlins' stadium at the same time the team was supposed to play a series against the Seattle Mariners. The concert could not be moved, so the Mariners hosted the Marlins in Seattle instead. Despite being almost 2,500 miles away from Miami, the Marlins were declared the "home team" for the three games.

WHICH MARLIN RECORDED THE TEAM'S MOST 'EXPLOSIVE' HIT?

LEGEND HAS IT that Luis Castillo did. It was his little foul pop against the Chicago Cubs in Game 6 of the 2003 NLCS—the one that led to eight runs and a pennant. A couple of months after the World Series, the ball was sold at a charity auction for more than $100,000. Did a lucky Marlins fan buy it? *No.* A Chicago restaurant owner bought the ball that cost the Cubs the pennant. He then had it blown to bits!

When a team begins a season by losing 22 of its first 38 games, the fans can usually expect a long, disappointing summer. Florida fans felt this way in 2003. The Marlins had one of the worst records in baseball. The team hoped to change its luck by replacing manager Jeff Torborg with Jack McKeon.

McKeon had been managing in the **big leagues** since the 1970s. He was known for keeping his team relaxed and giving young players a chance to learn. He also was not afraid to make big changes. In that lost season of 2003, McKeon seemed like the perfect man to help the young Marlins improve.

What happened next still has baseball people shaking their heads. McKeon handed the ball to his young pitchers—Dontrelle Willis, Brad Penny, Carl Pavano, Mark Redman, and Josh Beckett—and told them to go have some fun. He also called up Miguel Cabrera from the minor leagues. McKeon not only put the young star in the starting lineup, he asked him to move from third base to the outfield.

Every one of McKeon's moves seemed to work. Willis, who joined the team in May, found himself on the All-Star team in July! Cabrera hit a homer in his first game for the Marlins.

Jack McKeon celebrates with his team in 2003.

The Marlins started winning, and soon they set their sights on the playoffs. Florida piled up 18 victories in September—including wins in six of their last seven games—to become the NL Wild Card. It was an absolutely amazing comeback. Under McKeon, the Marlins went 75–49.

In the playoffs, Florida surprised the San Francisco Giants and Chicago Cubs. The Marlins next defeated the New York Yankees in the World Series. When the Manager of the Year award was announced that winter, no one was surprised—McKeon was the winner.

TEAM SPIRIT

One of the biggest changes in baseball in 2012 did not happen on the field. It happened in the seats at Marlins games. The team moved south to the city of Miami and made a new ballpark their home. At the same time, one of America's most diverse and exciting cities now has a new home team—it says so right on the caps and jackets worn by the fans and players!

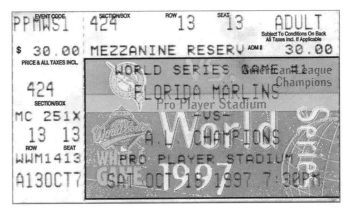

Loyal Marlins fans from years past are still in the stands cheering for the team. But now thousands of new fans—who had been unable to travel outside Miami—join them for every game. The team and the players feed off the energy of the city, and the city is buzzing about the Marlins' exciting young players.

LEFT: Florida fans count the number of strikeouts recorded by the Marlins' pitching staff during a playoff game in 1997. **ABOVE**: This ticket was good for a seat at Game 1 of the 1997 World Series.

TIMELINE

A.J. Burnett

1993
The Marlins finish their first season with a record of 64–98.

2001
A.J. Burnett pitches a no-hitter against the San Diego Padres.

1995
Quilvio Veras leads the NL in stolen bases.

1997
The Marlins win their first World Series.

2002
Luis Castillo has a 35-game hitting streak.

Moises Alou led the 1997 team with 23 homers.

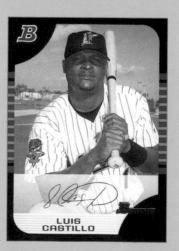

Luis Castillo

Dontrelle Willis was one of the team's top pitchers in 2003.

Josh Johnson

2003
The Marlins win their second World Series.

2009
Hanley Ramirez leads the NL in hitting.

2010
Josh Johnson leads the NL in ERA.

2006
Anibal Sanchez pitches a no-hitter.

2011
Gaby Sanchez is named an All-Star.

Anibal Sanchez celebrates his no-hitter.

Gaby Sanchez

FUN FACTS

JACK & MACK

In 2011, Jack McKeon became the second-oldest manager in big-league history at the age of 80. The oldest was Connie Mack, who managed until he was 87.

BIG FOUR

The 2006 Marlins had four rookie pitchers who won 10 or more games—Anibal Sanchez, Ricky Nolasco, Josh Johnson, and Scott Olsen. No team had ever done that before.

BIG THREE

The 2006 Marlins also had three rookies who hit 20 or more home runs—Dan Uggla, Josh Willingham, and Mike Jacobs. No team had ever done that before, either!

LUCKY NUMBER

In 2009, Gaby Sanchez became the fourth Marlins rookie to drive in six runs in a game. The first three were Charles Johnson, Mike Jacobs, and Cody Ross.

MR. PERFECT

In 1997, catcher Charles Johnson set a record by making no errors in 973 fielding chances.

HELP ME OUT, GUYS!

In 1996, Kevin Brown won 17 games and lost 11. The team scored a total of just 11 runs in those losses.

ONE FOR EACH FINGER

In 2010, Mike Stanton had five hits in a game. It marked the first time since the 1970s that a 20-year-old player accomplished this feat.

LEFT: Dan Uggla
ABOVE: Cody Ross

TALKING BASEBALL

"We have a lot of talent here. The new stadium, the weather ... I think I'm going to like it!"

▶ *JOSE REYES, ON JOINING THE MARLINS FOR THE 2012 SEASON*

"When I was coming up, I just wanted to play baseball. I'm doing what I love to do most."

▶ *MIGUEL CABRERA, ON THE THRILL OF BEING A BIG LEAGUER*

"I feel like I'm flying when I run the bases."

▶ *HANLEY RAMIREZ, ON TRYING FOR DOUBLES AND TRIPLES*

"I'm confident in myself. I've pitched big games all my life."

▶ *JOSH BECKETT, ON HIS APPROACH WHENEVER HE PITCHES*

"It's awesome to be from Miami and play for the Marlins because I was at the stadium as a little kid."

▶ **GABY SANCHEZ**, *ON THE PRIDE HE FEELS WHEN PUTTING ON A MARLINS UNIFORM*

"It's a mental test, a mental grind everyday."

▶ **MIKE STANTON**, *ON PLAYING IN THE BIG LEAGUES*

"There is a difference between an out and a productive out. There are situations where you need to make a **productive out**."

▶ **JIM LEYLAND**, *ON WHY A BATTER DOESN'T ALWAYS NEED TO GET A HIT TO HELP HIS TEAM WIN*

LEFT: Josh Beckett   **ABOVE**: Gaby Sanchez

GREAT DEBATES

People who root for the Marlins love to compare their favorite moments, teams, and players. Some debates have been going on for years! How would you settle these classic baseball arguments?

MIKE STANTON IS THE GREATEST SLUGGER IN TEAM HISTORY ...

MIKE
STANTON
FLORIDA MARLINS® OF

... because by the age of 21 he was already one of baseball's top power hitters. Stanton (LEFT) hit more than 50 home runs in his first two years with the Marlins. Neither season was easy for him. In 2010, Stanton got into only 100 games, but he still finished second on the club in home runs. In 2011, despite problems with his eyesight, Stanton managed to hit 34 homers to lead the team.

HE'LL HAVE TO SHOW HE'S BETTER THAN GARY SHEFFIELD FIRST ...

... because no one in the sport hit the ball harder than "Sheff." In 1996, Sheffield sent 42 balls over the fence for the Marlins. When the 2012 season started, that was still the team record. And speaking of eyesight, Sheffield not only hit for power, he had a good batting eye, too. The year he hit 42 homers, he also walked 142 times.

... because you need a mix of young stars and *veterans* to win a championship. The 1997 team had plenty of both. Kevin Brown, Al Leiter, Gary Sheffield, Moises Alou, and Bobby Bonilla (RIGHT) had years of wisdom and experience. They were amazing team leaders. Livan Hernandez, Edgar Renteria, Luis Castillo, and Robb Nen gave the team a special spark. They were good young players then, and most were still good 10 years later.

FORGET IT! THE 2003 MARLINS WOULD DESTROY THE 1997 MARLINS ...

... because good pitching stops good hitting. The 2003 team had tremendous talent on the mound. Josh Beckett, Brad Penny, Dontrelle Willis, Carl Pavano, Braden Looper, and Ugueth Urbina didn't give anyone a break. The New York Yankees had a team full of All-Stars in 2003, and yet they were able to win only two games in the World Series. When you add the speed and defense of the 2003 club, it is hard to see how the 1997 Marlins would even win one game!

FOR THE RECORD

The great Marlins teams and players have left their marks on the record books. These are the "best of the best" ...

Dontrelle Willis

Chris Coghlan

MARLINS AWARD WINNERS

WINNER	AWARD	YEAR
Livan Hernandez	NLCS MVP	1997
Livan Hernandez	World Series MVP	1997
Jack McKeon	Manager of the Year	2003
Dontrelle Willis	Rookie of the Year	2003
Ivan Rodriguez	NLCS MVP	2003
Josh Beckett	World Series MVP	2003
Hanley Ramirez	Rookie of the Year	2006
Joe Girardi	Manager of the Year	2006
Chris Coghlan	Rookie of the Year	2009

Livan
Hernandez

MARLINS ACHIEVEMENTS

ACHIEVEMENT	YEAR
NL Wild Card	1997
NL Pennant Winners	1997
World Series Champions	1997
NL Wild Card	2003
NL Pennant Winners	2003
World Series Champions	2003

ABOVE: In 2012, Tony Perez marked his 20th year as a member of the Marlins. He has served on the field as a coach and manager, and has also worked in the team's business office.
LEFT: Al Leiter was the team's starter in Game 7 of the 1997 World Series.

PINPOINTS

The history of a baseball team is made up of many smaller stories. These stories take place all over the map—not just in the city a team calls "home." Match the pushpins on these maps to the **TEAM FACTS**, and you will begin to see the story of the Marlins unfold!

TEAM FACTS

1. Miami, Florida—*The team has played in the Miami area since 1993.*
2. Oakland, California—*Dontrelle Willis was born here.*
3. Spring, Texas—*Josh Beckett was born here.*
4. Chicago, Illinois—*The Marlins won the 2003 pennant here.*
5. Tacoma, Washington—*Jeff Conine was born here.*
6. Blackwell, Oklahoma—*Brad Penny was born here.*
7. Mobile, Alabama—*Juan Pierre was born here.*
8. New York, New York—*The Marlins won the 2003 World Series here.*
9. North Little Rock, Arkansas—*A.J. Burnett was born here.*
10. San Pedro de Macoris, Dominican Republic—*Luis Castillo was born here.*
11. San Juan, Puerto Rico—*Mike Lowell was born here.*
12. Maracay, Venezuela—*Miguel Cabrera was born here.*

Mike Lowell

GLOSSARY

🧠 **ALL-STARS**—Players who are selected to play in baseball's annual All-Star Game.

🧠 **AMERICAN LEAGUE (AL)**—One of baseball's two major leagues; the AL began play in 1901.

🧠 **BIG LEAGUES**—The top level of professional baseball.

🧠 **CLUTCH**—Pressure situations.

🧠 *CONTRIBUTE*—Add to or strengthen.

🧠 *DECADES*—Periods of 10 years; also specific periods, such as the 1950s.

🧠 *DEFLECTED*—Changed the direction.

🧠 **EARNED RUN AVERAGE (ERA)**—A statistic that measures how many runs a pitcher gives up for every nine innings he pitches.

🧠 **FREE AGENTS**—Players who are allowed to join any team that wants them.

🧠 *LOGO*—A symbol or design that represents a company or team.

🧠 **MINOR LEAGUES**—The many professional leagues that help develop players for the major leagues.

🧠 **MOST VALUABLE PLAYER (MVP)**—The award given each year to each league's top player; an MVP is also selected for the World Series and the All-Star Game.

🧠 **NATIONAL LEAGUE (NL)**—The older of the two major leagues; the NL began play in 1876.

🧠 **NATIONAL LEAGUE CHAMPIONSHIP SERIES (NLCS)**—The playoff series that has decided the National League pennant since 1969.

🧠 **NL EAST**—A group of National League teams that play in the eastern part of the country.

🧠 **NO-HITTER**—A game in which a team does not get a hit.

🧠 **PENNANT**—A league championship. The term comes from the triangular flag awarded to each season's champion, beginning in the 1870s.

🧠 *PINSTRIPE*—Thin stripe.

🧠 **PITCHING STAFF**—The group of players who pitch for a team.

🧠 **PLAYOFFS**—The games played after the regular season to determine which teams will advance to the World Series.

🧠 **PRODUCTIVE OUT**—An out that scores a run or moves a runner to the next base.

🧠 *REPUTATION*—A belief or opinion about someone or something.

🧠 *RETRACTABLE*—Able to pull back.

🧠 **ROOKIE OF THE YEAR**—The annual award given to each league's best first-year player.

🧠 **RUNS BATTED IN (RBIs)**—A statistic that counts the number of runners a batter drives home.

🧠 *SCHOLARSHIP*—Financial aid given to a student.

🧠 **SHUTOUT**—A game in which one team does not score a run.

🧠 **STANDINGS**—A daily list of teams, starting with the team with the best record and ending with the team with the worst record.

🧠 *STRATEGY*—A plan or method for succeeding.

🧠 *VETERANS*—Players with great experience.

🧠 **WILD CARD**—A playoff spot reserved for a team that does not win its division, but finishes with a good record.

🧠 **WORLD SERIES**—The world championship series played between the American League and National League pennant winners.

EXTRA INNINGS

TEAM SPIRIT introduces a great way to stay up to date with your team! Visit our **EXTRA INNINGS** link and get connected to the latest and greatest updates. **EXTRA INNINGS** serves as a young reader's ticket to an exclusive web page—with more stories, fun facts, team records, and photos of the Marlins. Content is updated during and after each season. The **EXTRA INNINGS** feature also enables readers to send comments and letters to the author! Log onto:

www.norwoodhousepress.com/library.aspx

and click on the tab: **TEAM SPIRIT** to access **EXTRA INNINGS**.

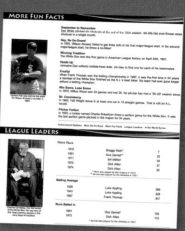

Read all the books in the series to learn more about professional sports. For a complete listing of the baseball, basketball, football, and hockey teams in the **TEAM SPIRIT** series, visit our website at:

www.norwoodhousepress.com/library.aspx

ON THE ROAD

MIAMI MARLINS
501 Marlins Way
Miami, Florida 33125
(877) 627-5467
miami.marlins.mlb.com

NATIONAL BASEBALL HALL OF FAME AND MUSEUM
25 Main Street
Cooperstown, New York 13326
(888) 425-5633
www.baseballhalloffame.org

ON THE BOOKSHELF

To learn more about the sport of baseball, look for these books at your library or bookstore:

- Augustyn, Adam (editor). *The Britannica Guide to Baseball*. New York, NY: Rosen Publishing, 2011.

- Dreier, David. *Baseball: How It Works*. North Mankato, MN: Capstone Press, 2010.

- Stewart, Mark. *Ultimate 10: Baseball*. New York, NY: Gareth Stevens Publishing, 2009.

INDEX

PAGE NUMBERS IN **BOLD** REFER TO ILLUSTRATIONS.

Alou, Moises.................6, 16, 26, **34**, 41

Beckett, Josh.........9, 18, 19, 21, 30, 38, **38**, 41, 42, 45

Bell, Heath...............................11

Boles, John................................24

Bonilla, Bobby........6, 16, 41, **41**

Brown, Kevin.....................6, 16, 17, **17**, 37, 41

Buehrle, Mark..........................11

Burnett, A.J.............7, 34, **34**, 45

Cabrera, Miguel.......9, 18, 22, **22**, 27, 28, **28**, 30, 38, 45

Castillo, Luis................7, 17, 18, 21, 26, 27, **27**, 29, 34, **34**, 41, 45

Clemens, Roger.........................21

Coghlan, Chris..................42, **42**

Conine, Jeff.....................6, **15**, 16, 20, 28, 45

Counsell, Craig............7, 17, 28

Daulton, Darren........................16

Fernandez, Alex....................6, 16

Girardi, Joe.......................24, 42

Gonzalez, Alex..........................19

Guillen, Ozzie...........................25

Hernandez, Livan.......7, 16, **16**, 17, 41, 42, **42**

Huizenga, Wayne........................7

Jacobs, Mike......................36, 37

Johnson, Charles.....6, 16, **17**, 37

Johnson, Josh..................**14**, 22, 35, **35**, 36

Lachemann, Rene......................24

Lee, Derek...........9, 18, **19**, 27

Leiter, Al...............6, 16, 41, **43**

Leyland, Jim................**16**, 17, 24, **24**, 39

Looper, Braden..................9, 41

Lowell, Mike..................9, 18, 21, **21**, 45, **45**

Mack, Connie...........................36

McKeon, Jack................18, 24, 25, **25**, 30, 31, **31**, 36, 42

Mordecai, Mike.........................27

Nen, Robb...................6, 16, 41

Nolasco, Ricky..........................36

Olsen, Scott.............................36

Pavano, Carl..........9, 18, 30, 41

Penny, Brad.....................7, 18, **18**, 30, 41, 45

Perez, Tony.............................**43**

Pierre, Juan...........9, **9**, 18, 19, 45

Ramirez, Hanley................**4**, **8**, 9, 23, **23**, 35, 38, 42

Redman, Mark..........................30

Renteria, Edgar...............7, **7**, 16, 18, 41

Reyes, Jose.......................11, 38

Rodriguez, Ivan.......9, 18, 27, 42

Ross, Cody.......................37, **37**

Ryan, Nolan..............................21

Sanchez, Anibal................9, 10, 35, **35**, 36

Sanchez, Gaby................**4**, 35, **35**, 37, 39, **39**

Sheffield, Gary.................6, **6**, 16, 20, 40, 41

Stanton, Mike.............10, **11**, 23, 37, 39, 40, **40**

Torborg, Jeff............................30

Uggla, Dan...................10, **10**, 23, 36, **36**

Urbina, Ugueth.........................41

Veras, Quilvio..........................34

White, Devon.......................6, 16

Willingham, Josh.......................36

Willis, Dontrelle.............9, 18, 22, 30, **35**, 41, 42, **42**, 45

ABOUT THE AUTHOR

MARK STEWART has written more than 50 books on baseball and over 150 sports books for kids. He grew up in New York City during the 1960s rooting for the Yankees and Mets, and was lucky enough to meet players from both teams. Mark comes from a family of writers. His grandfather was Sunday Editor of *The New York Times,* and his mother was Articles Editor of *Ladies' Home Journal* and *McCall's.* Mark has profiled hundreds of athletes over the past 25 years. He has also written several books about his native New York and New Jersey, his home today. Mark is a graduate of Duke University, with a degree in history. He lives and works in a home overlooking Sandy Hook, New Jersey. You can contact Mark through the Norwood House Press website.